WALKING THE BLIND DOG

Walking the Blind Dog

POEMS BY

G. E. Murray

UNIVERSITY OF ILLINOIS PRESS
Urbana and Chicago

Publication of this work was supported in part by a grant from the Illinois Arts Council, a state agency.

Manufactured in the United States of America
P 5 4 3 2 1

This book is printed on acid free paper.

Library of Congress Cataloging-in Publication Data

Murray, G. E., 1945–
Walking the blind dog : poems / by G.E. Murray.
p. cm.
ISBN 0–252–06231–0 (pb)
I. Title.
PS3563.U768W3 1992
811'.54–dc20 91-4138
CIP

For Joanne

First, at last, and
for the duration

Acknowledgments

Many of the poems collected here first appeared in the following publications:

Another Chicago Magazine: "Four Themes on a Variation," "At the Station Bar"
Antioch Review: "On Being Disabled by Light at Dawn in the Wilderness"
Ascent: "What the Waters Hold," "Never like This," "Three Children"
Birmingham Poetry Review: "Foreign Correspondence"
Chariton Review: "Swear to God: A Prologue from Memory"
Graham House Review: "The Body and Its Borders"
Hawaii Review: "On Getting Unstuck"
Hudson Review: "Midwinter Love Lyric"
Louisville Review: "The Repossessions"
Mississippi Valley Review: "The Riverbank Potentials"
Montana Review: "On Being Out There," "On Being Out Here"
Northwest Review: "Haunts," "Satisfaction Guaranteed or Your Emotions Cheerfully Refunded" (originally published as "Persuasions")
The Ohio Journal: "Crossings: November 21-22"
Open Places: "The Squaw Trade"
Overture: "Looking toward Peoria"
Poetry: "Flying Low, near France, among Birds," "Northern Exposures"
Poetry Northwest: "For Drunks, in the Nighttime"
Prairie Schooner: "The Rounds"
Seneca Review: "Double-Dare Dreams at the Hotel Amsterdam," "At the Tifft Street Dump"
Sewanee Review: "Walking the Blind Dog"
Southern Humanities Review: "A Year's Time, Its Music Baroque as Cancer"
South Florida Poetry Review: "Thanksgiving Snakes," "On Laying Keel"
TriQuarterly: "At the Japanese Baths"
Anthology of Magazine Verse and Yearbook of American Poetry: "Northern Exposures"

I wish to express gratitude to the Illinois Arts Council for grants that helped me complete this book.

Contents

FIRST

Swear to God: A Prologue from Memory

Lately, this mistake of a breeze congeals blue tons
Around me—vague waters
And persuasions of September growing too obvious
To be convenient; tracts
Within a tract where I hover among old particulars:
A vanilla-nougat sky
Becoming twilight, bleating of scows, everything
Underfoot gone soft.
I make small talk with shadows guiding me downwind;
I carry on with it,
The novelty of traveling this far on sympathy alone.
It can't be my silences;
Tonight, there are others: wash of harbor home,
This vacuum of earnings
And works I call autobiography. Behind wood railings
I am one avid stranger,
Profile of an unheard drumroll suspended in winks
Of forgetfulness, wave
Of hands: nothing but traces the failing light
Chooses to make orange
Like autumn, blurred and cooling. I want for birdsong
And get instead a gull.
Hapless in its outward climb, speck on the skyline,
At last just hanging there
With difficulty. This is another hour, serious time.
Any moment I could prove
How sad it is to gather scattered pieces of occasions;
How monologue soon turns
Full circle for meaning. A long draw of breath keeps
The match alive, as night
Solidifies in a heap. I look differently. Time away
Can't fix a history
As you would have it, with treatise and dislocation,
Yet so much at home,
Stalking comforts of instincts I know far less about.

Like a mousetrap sprung
By larger game, a queer emptiness creates this space,
The scarcity of life
Shut in it, forever checked and held. I stare out,
Sweeping for echoes,
Those familiar piers that manhandle imagination,
A lyric like a wand
Slowly passing over my bones. In the same cold way,
I heel to whatever
Unravels in the digest of night fog, and it starts:
Aroma of Friday night's
Yellow or blue pike fried crisp in dockside saloons,
Delicious once more,
Wafting among the unshaven men from rented rooms,
Who sink downstairs
To stumble in sawdust. People I know are here.
I hear them dissecting
Ambitions and love, those bloodless crimes of self
They tell in clusters,
In muscatel voices. The jukebox scratches on and on.
The sauntering proceeds;
Punctual calls for more watered liquor and song
All night. With such music,
Such wallowing of entertainments, they celebrate
Minor natural disasters—
Wasting no words, braced for the last swallow.
Halfway home to memory's
Free clinic, an exercise in redemptions, and it's me
Again, really sliding up
A crowded, beer-soaked floor, and I'm six years old
Again, and I'm dancing
For heartless laughs and a fistful of gray pennies,
By God, dancing hard.

SECOND

What the Waters Hold

There exists within the United States and Canada—principally between longitudes 76° west and 92° west and between latitudes 41° north and 49° north—a region in which several hundred peculiar events have been recorded. The concentration of such events is far greater than any random statistical dispersion would normally place within these boundaries. The principal geographic features of this region are five freshwater lakes.

—Gourley, *The Great Lakes Triangle*

Each lake often shows a definite personality. Superior is male: cold, moody, mysterious. Michigan is female: generally friendly, sometimes very warm, but often squally. Huron is a back-country pitchman: shallow, a bit commercial, and far more dangerous than it appears. Lake Erie is ambivalent: very shallow and always verging on trouble. . . . At the far eastern end there's Ontario, lowest of the lot, closest to the ocean, and perhaps for this reason seemingly different from the others.

—McKee, *Great Lakes Country*

1 Superior

To mix with time and the weather
ahead, and this ceremonial sunset
linking wicker chair

to gangplank. By whaleback steamer
it's 383 miles westerly
from Chapel Rock to the pine-knot fires

taunting heavyweight
Canadian nights. Along the way,
you press rough waters

beyond shadow play and toppling
rain on driftwood, the dead stalks
of sunflower wavering

further, beyond occasional farms,
lights snapping on for a late supper
or something else. As if pursuing

connection with landfall,
however indistinct, you guess
how to relinquish words,

how to manage and continue, naming
again a nightwatch less human
than hearth or duck blind:

these cold peculiarities
of unrecorded event—say,
the shore-bound properties of duckweed

and spiderwort, sirens
of grackle, junco, and snow bunting
above. In the far North Woods,

you contrive an old scheme
for salvage. Then you watch to listen
where you fade in the dawn light,

as a freighter passes into fog bank,
disappearing, its bell-moan
forever calling you to follow now.

2 Michigan

A fetch of wind bums up from prairie.
        So it catches a mushroom hunter in the act

of selecting his rare morels. So it prods
        old women heavy with plastic shopping bags,

who flee Chicago before daybreak like mice.
        So it flutters these fine ornamental waters,

so incautious, irregular, and comely—
        ever alive with a marriage of freedoms.

And gulls always hover the birth of any season,
        flanking each other, diving to separate hungers.

Forgive us this dream of black and white,
        of the sad grins of the smelt fishermen,

that fast dancing in lakefront casinos,
        of blowtorch stacks rimming a lower skyline,

of kickwater shells gathering to design,
        of the chalky galactic light warming like milk

over Shedd Aquarium, along Meigs Field,
        inflexible in habit, without good reason.

We believe somehow in a northern shore,
        where the pig-iron barge trundles outward

toward movie-house darkness, and one gull
        lifts slowly and high in its losing flight.

3 Huron

Suddenly snow comes rowing over
Bay City, East Saginaw,
Pinconning, these raw elbows

Dipping again to chafing tests of ice.
The plank sidewalks respond
With aches and a tonnage all their own.

By any eastern view, even briefly,
The lake's dull percussion
Rattles the wind of the mainstream

You absorb, the few days you sold
From a life gone past wishing.
Nothing too spectacular.

What we bear, what we contain,
Is out there twitching like antennae,
Revolving, going down.

In time, more snow catches on,
Shrinking on contact,
Small measures of replenishment.

And here the town huckster
Shoots pool alone,
Knowing the lake wins everything.

For a moment, from shrill distance,
You see in the bottlenecked
Village traffic a sign: *Danger:*

Men Working in Trees.
Not here. Not in winter. Only
A chainsaw on the ground waiting

To be pulled alive; only
A tool belt left like a gauntlet,
Unanswered, while all over

The snow ferries us to a year's
New landing, and obscures
What demise these waters hold.

4 Erie

for Gus Stavrou

Sometimes it plays a troubled anthem
Or blinks awake to morning with a hush,

Hungover from indiscretions and lessons
Never taught. It can't hurt here,

Even with seiche, for a breeze pulling back
This sheeted water won't show

The sludge worms or soils leaching out.
It's deep green now, quiet, inhaling sky.

In rare sun and second wind, our times lost
Remain as abrasions suffered in sleep,

A secret grit eating away the hold of bricks.
At Point Abino, timid sail craft weave

An indelible calligraphy, tack on
Faith and shallow accommodation. Whatever

Of tomorrow will be told in nuisance,
In cloudy dispersions of industry

Swimming up the wind's black track to Niagara.
In a downtown Buffalo hotel, a man

Bereaved of comfort and lakeview
Loses all but his immaculate eye

For this place of little fame
And questionable depth that fills him.

5 Ontario

This is how it is in the desert
but with lowland backwaters—
always April, a chilled amber sky

moving in pieces. Past guesswork
and the idea of a fragrant,
pelting rain, past all fanfare

for the distinctive waters reeling
into Canada and permanence
elsewhere, this afternoon speaks

to itself in the patois of loss.
Within the slightest song
of finch and fox sparrow, among

other warnings out of sight, a clean
parlay of currents muster
to cool another hunting season,

another day given to stoop-labor.
I know the flow of eelgrass
is a constant, sheltered mishap

from the land's echo and contagion.
I know this sweet water-logged
rot, the spawning of desire

unattainable. This is how a desert
shrouds us, in the kelp
of sunlight, a radiance yellowing

like certain flowers and teeth.
I move bone-tired to cradle
benefits of my doubt, pretending

to become soft and buoyant.
Whether or not the new spillways
clog, that time someone offered

love on a dare, in a borrowed skiff,
remains, as do I, in freshwater,
confidant to these darker seasons.

THIRD

Never like This

for the father and child

It was never like this, a random text
Laid open to hourly confessions
Heard there in that afternoon blackening
Like a suture. Never as I suspected,
Our stock remembering,
Promissory times of a father
And child gone hunting as if they should,
Deaf to their disarrays, extracted
From an alchemy of trust like pure metals.
Then they show up one winter in a blind,
A clutch of manners and surprise,
Calling out for company, some news
From the child soon upon them.
They wait for a break in December's weather,
Feeding like pigeons on the snow's crust.
They know just how far they have come
Now, resolving their own beginnings in fact.

The Rounds

for my father (1917-81)

The dark changes guard
With the Swiss-blue hardware of morning.
So the world and its debts are spitshined once more.

But nothing so alive and loyal
As the single light kept lit all night in the pantry—
Our best provisions slightly out of reach.

Nothing so killing
As the sudden parentheses of your years
As I sprawl here mourning,
A fast-moving idea, finally, come home.

It is Fourth of July and the music's
Strummed down and up my spine,
Long-playing tunes of a burial time.

It's the rounds again, so cheers—
Your prizefights, secret whiskies, the blood-love
I learned like a hardwood burn.

Only your favorite god knows
I buy no news about you,
Save the practical
Demonstration of your death.

My brother, my mother told me so, told true:
Death on the holiday, death at noon.

With the last of your peach brandy,
I salute us and the icy light in the pantry.

And already I learn to settle for more

* * *

No dawn ever comes back.
No others need apply.
No more the irrigated life.
No final instructions.

I huddle here colder and clear,
Reinventing everyone
In first sunlight's streaming dust,
Remembering things whole

And unbloodied, in chiaroscuro.
Thus, I hardly know where to begin
This hemorrhaging, this life
As gorgeous as your heart.

Your absence floods. Being solitary
Becomes the matter and the affirmation
Of good gray soul in turnabout.
But we both knew we knew that:

One man's shining idol, another's
Spittoon. Also, the first ending: you
Dying in the middle of a sneeze,
Slumping back to a black fuss,

Shot through like a fuse
Exploded in its socket, a pain
Now made precisely important
And perfect as a child's love.

In those sold, latter days,
What was in us still turned lyrical.

Yet our stories altered by the month;
Each utterance, a suction

Of solitude and foul weather,
Even now new proving grounds.
Keep the weep out of the voice.
Nay-say the night, its aspirations.

Ah, but we traveled mostly at night,
Lucky to be so lost
To our gigantic businesses,
None of which will ever miss us.

I aped the traveling man,
Loved this and that, surely,
Chasing after rounds of your life.
Now I no longer make them.

* * *

Let me get this right
Or let me be wrong again and again and again
With my dry reachings, resolute,
Determined as mahogany not to splinter.
I come this far on sincere condolences:
No rescue there, no outstanding issues.
Simply the necessary languages of the dead.
Simply time given over to time;
One more lasting, invisible snow.
It only returns to this: a stammering
That's the east wind; a harsher wind
That's love in its outwash. Funny how it works
On the bullet-proof, those of us
Certified as anvils.
One time late in the pressing twilight
Of hardball times,

You half-berserk on work's edge,
And me stuck with more stories of my near-drowning,
You went hot-eyed, tear-drunk
For your far-gone father, still psychedelic
Against mill flame, mule-backed, forever stoking
Furnace and the beauty of the literal.
You were chasing his light.
You were becoming it.
You knew then that last fierce
Loving touch we Irish reserve for the dead,
Long before that Swiss-blue morning
I changed guard with your darks.

A Year's Time, Its Music Baroque as Cancer

What dear things are nearly held safest
In their hushed becomings
Before rumors run to fat,
Sour in sun, or go blind
From scum like canal water?
So time sometimes whirls off its sprockets.
Sometimes your own meat spoils
On the shank. And we tap out the wrong music,
A piece cut loose to the general wind.
By night, the high wires whine and tell
Your story in clutching, stoney mist.
Even then, flint, touched, gives no spark;
A woman, touched, gives no warmth.
The violet summer empties
Instantly, through palms cupped in prayer.
Winter soon drums into the finest of your bones.

Three Children

Three children rocking on a porch of Sundays,
A vacation wind quickening them
Into blue nudes. By the pact of midday sun,
They resemble the instant
Before lightning splits an elm in pieces.

No, thank you, they resemble nothing
But warming domes on the afternoon dreamless
As sand in their play shoes. They doubt
Any animal they ride could pretend
Beyond lessons of exquisite balance
Or sure pastimes of transport. They remain
Lotions pouring everywhere.

As if from time to time they sit at the center
Of running lights, in some boat, gathering
Smiles in a spray of unearthly attention,
This scene is curtained, kept moving

Finally by the beacon of a single train
Their father once saw rumble
Through a childhood far away. They are
Young sleepers on that train,
Sharing a preferred berth between stations,
Bearing down, gusting like a blast from air brakes,
Too soon to vanish.

A jay flies up to where they were just rocking.
It knows we are like them.

Thanksgiving Snakes

Immaculate year, and someone between storms
Visits again the routines of November's gulch.

* * *

It's clear, this day in the coming dark,
Where you see everything featured in mist,
Caring more to stalk after a curiosity of light
Set back in landscape's old upholstery—
A light unassigned to house or hunter,
Only this lost idea of blue spark popping off . . .

* * *

It was afternoon on a ceremonious walk home
Alone with a body's reluctant pleasures,
Conceiving hard-packed ingredients
Of dream, as strong as fear left unnoticed
In marsh, newly rotting,
While the gawk-gawk of loon pushed out
From this small recess of field,
A flooded rut. Only the Iron Works,
Backed against salty edges
Of canal water, answered in service
Of bleached spaces, elementary cloud schemes.

Down Tonawanda Road, downhill
Once more, trampling a stray white bud
Out of season, as if thunder in winter,
Then crashing off hog-like into barbed brush
And water-borne ooze, mucking out
Through the last few high reeds
For sport, for the child-still-feeling,
While hoarfrost and air
Turned delicate as a dancer's wrist.

* * *

How unfortunately far away the unstuck frogs;
How much fun to spill blood as if oil on water;
And then to sink upon creek mud
Where tadpoles first scattered in spring,
That mud the balm of a hundred scrapes.
But now I think more of high-back chairs
And holiday feast, steam gathering
Inside windows, chimneys smoking
Yellow on the soon-to-be ignored horizon . . .

Yet here, a warning hush through saplings,
A sure drop in temperature.
And I journey back among clutter—
Pitching stones at a soup-can home
For worms, able to pick my crusty nose in peace.
And I burst a little farther,
Over double ditches, beyond the kickball lot,
Nearer an Erie & Lackawanna trestle,
Up above cuts of second-growth birch,
When—What?—a sudden thrashing of shadow
Strikes and wraps its ferocious body-muscle
Long to my leg and heart-fright,
My sad canvas shoe.

* * *

I stomped that hunger hard until we both went limp.
I raced to pile wet earth and difference between us.

* * *

Until home again. Dry again. A warm drink
And the compound riches of table being set.
My father whispering at his book;
Mother presiding at the stove's goodness;
The family awaiting giblets

On this night like eiderdown,
As we begin to devour bird,
From flesh to its tender, broken neck.

The Repossessions

How the running sky means to summarize
The companions of our lives;
How another sunrise buries them
Again in simple truths. Now,
It's a fascination with Northern Lights
Maybe, waiting out the horizon
With a handful of jonquils
In some roadside bar, blaming
Lessons of the heat
On another summer's dried husk.

Why is it only tonight
The infinite dead you love
Turn reasonable again—
Their blue shores blending
With dusk's solvent blush,
Reaching off to where you were,
Configuring in ideal air,
All that's going, what's truly gone?

Tonight, only the dead you love
Ordain the places you left,
Lacking any right connection
Or vast territorial caress.
Only those dead you love tonight
Reach out like floodlights,
Grow louder than anthems.
So we have intricate times told
In two-part harmony, our retreats
And crossings, cold drizzle.
So we hold this rolling stock
Of adult provisions, desert of kin
On the brink of some history,
More tombs. You know how it is,
The rummagings, that texture

Of a night simply starved
And forever possessed.

The only dead you love tonight
Beg for small maintenance
Of soul, huddle within eyeshot
Of water's simplicity,
That circular pass
Of a lengthening beacon.
Only then you'll know what's known
About the true bearings
Of those dead you love tonight;
Then only you can continue
Changing back, coming forth.

Foreign Correspondence

You report yet another war from the same hotel bar,
alive to familiar toothaches
and the high, hard issues
of that green-eyed woman upstairs
who never turns out her lights

in time. Once again men with unhealed tattoos
invent a history for the ages,
while you persist in displaying
bad manners in holy places,
insisting upon a heavy rewrite
of character, albeit truthful and downright.

You record the installation of intemperance,
subscribe to a ground-floor competence,
using the dispatch as bullet, an unkind word
as faith. And you know out of troubled dreaming
comes the huge ragtag rush and procession
of nights when you stare deepest
into native eyes and see the world once more
surviving its own instincts.

Say you get sick of hot winds blowing north,
the children with flies in their mouths.
To the uneasy, softening heart,
you say, if you can't win the game,
upset the chess board. You say,
to prevent madness, pop a blood vessel.

Just as soon as you go hawking or stalking
a perfect tolerance for the dimples of goodness,
you know how your famous hotel bar
goes dark, inexplicably, limiting choices
of disapproval. Perhaps some bombings
tonight? Or maybe the utility went unpaid?

Whatever, it's you and your love
of daily bedlam, strong drink and tobacco
staring back from the barroom mirror,
through the crystal decanters darkly,
the barman conveniently gone, the night
another ruin, morning simply a fear,
as you begin speaking intimately
with all that must remain invisible.

At the Station Bar

Here, for an instant, stands God's empty seat,
Pivot to nearly all five-cornered arguments
You survived while drinking in all this darkness
At the Victoria Station bar.

Where's God, you ask, off pissing
Off the usual sniffs again?

A focus to this undistinguished winter night
And to your seasonal drooling,
Preseminal, as you flag
Every odd woman stopping by, beautiful
And brilliant, each as if a teardrop.

You're swimming in cash and gravity and shade.
But you haven't a prayer.
And it's too late to become an answer
To your own resurrection.

In the name of God and one eye
Of the timely station master—
Both emphatic as ice—
You don't like deciding between what's wonderfully
Right or wrong with London these days,
With the effect of rain on wool,
With the caviar crowd,
Or occasional legs warming
Around your waist.

And you've missed another train on the Baker-Loo line,
If only to hear of more lost callings,
If only to keep faith as you advance home by inches,
At half-staff, bloodshot, and tasting of dusk-blue.

Fear and brightness have been struck down once more.
You slip onto the wrong train
Toward the Embankment. God's with you again.

At the Tifft Street Dump

You might as well take that penny out to the rails
and let a train flatten it,

if you want to play it so close to your toenails.
That's life in the dumps. That's knowing trash

happens in the spirit of memory's hot gash.
Trackside, sweating out the cold,

near the end of a line, you vanish back
into muck for one gracious moment,

all your hazards exactly right. Hunkered,
you remember why the wind has skills, eh?

How it is again to work the high weed cover,
cutting low, in slow stalking,

deliberate and unstoppable as sludge,
before rising as if a deer first hearing winter

snap alive. Slip alongside the rotted siding
tonight, embrace the glass-strewn fields.

Wander toward the old coupling-house,
forever with your love of rust and reckonings,

a temporary order. You may play until dark
if only to keep in touch with your timing

on loose gravel, that famous crossover step
you used to jump freights as they crept

to shrill cries over so much scrap metal.
Don't make it a strange thing.

It's coming on to blow and darkening fast.
You're home now, and starting to die.

Buffalo, New York

At the Japanese Baths

Unconditionally undressing,
swaying to Kabuki tunes,

and this early evening blending
with soap and herbal steam,
as if uncertain bloods

while the two of us enter
tiled rooms on a slant.

Idly, stretched out in suds, I remember
last night at Kitcho restaurant
I spent too many yen
and heard a local industrialist joke:
"Nagasaki was an old town, anyway."

Chop-chop.
Stand for wash
of ribcage, waist, thigh,
and honor. Our thoughts
push on, pull off,
heat rising between
probes of another ancient dawn
and this comforting
of a modern itch.

It's the nearness of her
fine knuckles
digging my collarbone
for pinpoint truths
I won't surrender
in aftermath

to either goosebumps
or heartworm . . .

A gaffed fish,
she hauls me naked to her table
forty years after The Bomb.

Shall we get on with our silences?

Lowering,
she knows bones
hot and distant
as stars.

Toweled off,
I lay on my back
close to joy
and her tiny,
intelligent knees,
raised to art,
as we translate
a dialog of grunts,
deep as that.

So it is whenever I prize her precise feet
bodywalking, I dream
she must be marching hard
into the foothills of Fuji
one moonless night,
us both bone-white and filled
with mist and stoney ash

from the very times we survive,
obedient to pain,
attendant to withdrawal,

while neither would ever admit
feeling a thing.

Tokyo

FOURTH

The Squaw Trade

According to local belief, Squaw Island—which is situated in the midst of the Niagara River near Buffalo, New York—was home for a band of prostitutes who serviced workers from the Erie Canal, circa 1840. Today, Squaw Island is a municipal refuse dump for the city of Buffalo.

1

Slime burlap on timbers riverside, yea
More captive berths to consider: boundaries
Set by familar propositions
Of comfort and flatbottom mud. We men
Haul up some miracle of a ditch
To what's called Squaw Island.
And such remains the canalman's trade
At last. Harsh ways, we tell you,
Woman, your eyes and rapture averted
To the long boats pulled in tandem
To your door. How could we see then
How it was always us alone—
Unknown stations in need of poor launch?

2

If they could sing or even listen
A little, we'd be lost deep in the pitch
And rumble of real lives, primed
To unload a pledge or two of return.
One day, under the shadow of hawks,
We locked in the long grass
As if slugs. The aftermath was quick
Parting, forever maybe, then back
To our stories of the packet boat
Whacking through tangle reeds
And the stoop-backed Irish turning mythic
In this, a speechless country,
Almost mysterious as perfume itself.

3

Captivated at Little Falls, gone clean
By Weedsport, pressing toward
Those vainglorious times up in Lowertown
Where we'd stroll the day, liquor
In hand, waiting a turn at the Locks.
It should be allowed as how girls
Were not forgotten, either. Sure
In any faint light setting off-island,
You see the hair's worn from their legs
By woolen trousers. Odd why
Such standard gossip keeps us
Huddled around cigar smoke and fun,
Ever shuffling, ready again to move soon.

4

After miles of stumps and clear-cut skies,
More stumps. And the deadly matter
Of building country in the calm of summer
Burdens like a search for much worse.
Thinking through a warm afternoon rain,
Thinking of getting there, downwater
Toward neglect for glory's sake
And other never-lasting bounty,
A blessing, it seems, becomes this—
All passages so unworldly hot
As to be bitter, our own massive bones
Sweating. O Motherly touch and need,
What have we to do with thee?

5

Just nervous, and the skirtless brides
Seem just the same. At the taking
Of shore, there's care for the prize
Portraiture of a girl at sixteen in your vest,
Driving you mad, and on. It's a gravity
In the blood, unchangeable as the waif
You are, a dwarf among dwarfs, no force.
They tell you they understand. So half
The time so drunk as to see, you wear
Your life like a bandanna. That's all
Nobody's business. That's all the secret
There is. But to any woman's edges,
Rubbed soft as landscape, you are less.

6

Kissing that last sure drop of sweat
From a heavy lip, tongues wag easy
In this good composted land
Amid mire and flesh, a threat of snow.
We rise from a hut born
To game and holiday, knowing barely
Ourselves. None of us escape
The terrible progress we make
Suffering yet another pleasure.
Sad, say, the ways we loved like stones—
No courting dance, no feathers
Or gesture. But then nobody asked
For more than favors or strange luck.

7

They watch for clouds. Any muster
Could ruin business, however damp
Already the shining caves that bristle
Like pearl in moonlight. Beneath their belts
The sources of circumstance and invention
Turn nightfall to a wash. Lacking
A westerly push toward Erie, the hide
Tingles for a pressure, a sign,
If only the whine of a full day's water
Lost to Niagara. In fair time,
The swell might thicken and warm
As soup in the casual hands
Of a visitor aging to unwelcome weathers.

8

So it's Buffalo: gutspill and sideshow,
Crusade of rascals swaggering
Up Front Street. Lovey, it all passes forth—
The heart's infirmities, our grinding
Labors. . . . Who hasn't spent a life
Making civilization right and not
Gone wrong? Soon there'll be other empires,
Then farther west, further refinements
Of the breed. We conclude here,
A rainy frontier, end of a pity. What's more?
Ah, dreaming, we'd scheme of strangers
Above our sorry place, wise builders erecting
Able love some hundred years hence!

9

Like a hatch of horseflies streaming
Into gray light, we've grown free to cross
The flushing river on abundant piping
Of sludge. Where's the barrelhouse,
The waste of laughter and bile that releases?
Instead there's a world piled on bedrock,
A history failing its horizons,
Properties of muck increased by modern
Wealth. We're where the lost bodies
Of unshared spheres intertwine
As a distant rescue from style and form,
From tales left squalid in the telling:
Now just a vigilance, faith's fallen banner. . . .

FIFTH

Flying Low, near France, among Birds

I'm coming in right on line from Lille.
I'm veering far south beyond attention,
Focusing low and tight on a blue stain
Of innocence there on a bronze cheek.
I'm coming down with something now,
Indications of the usual, a soft yawn,
Night relief, making most of disattachments,
While yielding to speech on an evening
With anything else but the last light out.
I'm still coming in on line from Lille,
And everywhere fresh contours, everywhere
There are glimpses of the delicious
In a losing struggle against bad air,
Womb of clouds. Faster, from Lille,
I'm punching huge holes through filament,
Gaining time on that beacon just off the jetty.
I'm hugging up and bloomed soon enough,
A late diver, learning to turn smack
Into the flight of a hawk, arriving worthwhile,
Stranger among perfumes and tailfeathers.

Northern Exposures

for Richard Hugo

You hear the roadhouse before you see it,
Its four-beat country tunes
Amplified like surf through the woods,
Silencing bullfrog and red-tailed hawk,
Setting beards of moss dancing
On dim, indeterminate trees
That border two-lane blacktop.
Docked tonight, you reveal the badge
Of the farmer, that blanched expanse of skin
Where cap shades face, babyhood
Pallor above the sun-blackened jaw
Bulging uneasy with a concrete grin
And some inevitable need to weep.
Don't you think we live and breathe
In the meantime, in lockstep
With dawn, sunset, brawling dawn?
Even now, you await secrets worse
Than the few known ways a seized sky
Will come to survive your pity.
But on another far field, celebrated
For its arrivals and evictions, you learn
To be beautiful, never leading
A sensible life, playing ball in the early dark,
Fighting for a taste of the sweet spot,
In this uncut land, this straight-edged air.
Whadya want to know that isn't yet a mystery
Somewhere, a confidential stumble, heat
Lightning, a first-rate backseat turndown?
So it is that later you track high above
Familiar tamarack and ash, beginning
The next inaccuracy alone, and again,
Remembering that everything east of you
Has already happened, on the same cold ground,

In a swarm of time, finally spiked home
To your surprise, nails flung to the air.
And us all thumbs to the hot hammer-licks
You hear from the roadhouse before you see it.

On the Train to Dubuque

The old woman asks about penguins
Rehearsing all that day
On the ridge over the Apple River.

In paling light, she knows illusion
When she abuses it,

Already confusing trackside events
For acts of importance.
In the dark molding of late October,

High piles of winesaps and pumpkins
Rot in the dignity
Of their own fields, unexplained.

Nearing Pearl City
And its fool dream of culture's
Entanglements, a few black power lines

Run overhead and unobstructed
As if drawn taut by a weight of landscape.

There are no stories now to hold onto
Like riding straps, no real
Amusements unveiled in reflections

Racing across chrome, speeding
Against the melancholy
Of this righteous cool cave of evening

Curving into view. Minutes away
From the hillside neon welcome
Of *Bluff Tap and Liquors,*

One more glance at the burr
Clinging to an old woman's sundress,
The distances of an old woman
Never getting off.

Looking toward Peoria

July's scythe levels air.
What season must we become, what
Thrush singing in its song.

The bold phrasing of cornfields
Articulates nothing
But a westward leaning.
Beginning simply
With embraces and limits,
Something soon must tell us
What grows in the cold,
What requires
—in neat parenthesis—
Our bones.

After supper
All talk is incidental
And straight
As a rural road.
When we take to front-porch
Fiddling, we stir
Murmurs of distance:

A leaf in millstream;
Two miles of boxcars
Chasing fast for home.

The Riverbank Potentials

for Laurence Lieberman

Another walk down to the boathouse,
Watchful of snares
And blue lights flickering further out.
And an oddly modern figure rises
From a long night crouched
On something like limestone,
Peat flat or rucksack,
To audition a dream of tidal water
Through the green gum of one eye.
And here just stones and wisteria
Make esplanade enough
For the irregular passing of patrols.
What else should I tell you?
The last boat out there, beyond
Blackberry thorn and quarry,
Lists near the emptying station.
It's a child's boat, a skiff
Wrecked from age
Or long-awaited stoning . . .

The local swimmers meanwhile
Continue sleeping alone, twisting
Among sheets and approximations
Of past rescues as they
Slide half in or out
From a skin's lenient darkness.
I'll miss this, the ruins of shore,
Old stonework all along
The savannah, the escarpment. That
And the river's hidden fork;
That, and a lack of complication
Beginning in the far north . . .

Now it's the harvest moonrise,
Now open season on favorite songbirds.
But the borders are not unfair,
Only far. At each scenic bend and then
Each farewell, the silver track
Of river changes current over slab-rock.
And later, the mudbanks come alive
By flashlight, a length of something old
Slipping from covered canoe
Into the shed of unrealized night;
Several cottonmouths following.
That was how the swimmers knew
Where to dive for tokens
Of relief and opportunity
In the prologue of downriver gray,
To locate that one satin place
Where love learns to plunge under
Without pardon, ripple, or gasp.

Midwinter Love Lyric

Up through Waterville Notch, gone raw for hours
On speechless white plain
Of ice-cloud, anchored in snow; through basin
And pass and glimmer, backward
Into a crosshatched weave of shore's insignia,
Where the early pitch of darkness easily fills
Our tracks, our ways of digging in.
Still, we surely know silhouette
From our yearly unlearning, high ground
From echo. At this range the benevolent sight
Of a steeplejack watching us
Localizes spectre, idiom, and feature,
Makes for a good, gray, government sky
Hovering in witness of these musical surfaces.

So much for earth's clean muscle,
And the first afternoon of a season
That sours in all black corners of a squall.
This is the only welcome we entertain:
Shortcomings of path, tongues warming
To a pause for brittle conversation,
Star talk. We break off what we can
And call it deadly shivers. Beginning *now*.

Satisfaction Guaranteed or Your Emotions Cheerfully Refunded

after Django Reinhardt

Love took your teeth
One wet day on the boulevard.
Love shook itself free
As a goose in the brasserie.
Like some inch of you,
A glitter
In all this concealment,
Things might get swift tonight.
So lie down in me, please,
One luxurious moment
As we swell like curves,
like hurdy-gurdy times.
There are indications;
Technical healings
Akin to infancy.
In wintertime I work
At what warmth remains,
Caught up in scarves,
Single-minded as an insect.
You leave three times,
Like the rain, only to return
With a fleck of blood
On your lip. What's to gain
By going public with this?
Tell me from the start
What you saw and what you
Think it means: A future
Of virtue, missed callings,
The wanton husk.
We commingle like taxis,
Racing darkly
To each new confection.
Butter your bread

Curbside, smilingly.
Return to love toothless.
Certainly, that was
This: A last insinuation,
Then a change of neighborhood.

On Being Disabled by Light at Dawn in the Wilderness

Sight seems colored by the hour,
Sucked up through the trees' capillary fans,
Streaking out to sunlight well-kept: marsh-red morning,
Pale blue at noon, the connubial warmth
Of lemon with a late sun and, later, always
Black disapproving black, there in the middle of love.

Yet how beautiful when submitted fully to hungers
Of time breaking into you, as if sitting alone
In a room when glass cracks, necessarily unexplained.
First sight again, light's dispensations
At dawn, segue to all you volunteer
And preserve of the uninvestigated dream.

Forget remembering what fear has loved.
I wake to you and the morning that has come up
Crystal, its facets endlessly reflective, nearly
Deathless, but dying nonetheless, and so,
Undefinable as luck, which cautions:
Do not harden in light; occur only in ecstasy.

Boulder Junction, Wisconsin

On Laying Keel

As if this wound was nearing completion,
The brawn of it, the brain of it. . . .

I would power into pine
Until I became pine-edged,
A spasm spent by moonlight,
Then I would buck and shudder
To the instructions of pine
Becoming backbone for us both.

Out on the Ways,
Working on the wombstone
Of what will be lost eventually
To ocean's thrift,
I set another trendline,
Extend appendage,
Defy what's cockeyed
To set courses straight.

All the black winter
This bitch of a wind punches holes
Up river and me.
It's the wind's participation
In process. It's my content.

I rely upon the shipbuilder's dominion
For all my cunning stunts.
I thaw as well when spring stalls,
The blood running again,
Corrosion in the air,
The sudden pulse of pine
Whipsawed and tamed, cradled alive,
So blessed, far and away,

As if this healing was never ending.

On Getting Unstuck

at San Francisco Airport

A real pea-souper,
As if our Limehouse Days,
Us singing a mantra of retreat,
Grounded tonight by an outlying fog,
The predatory link of your disattachments,
Idled here, dead-heading at the worst of times.

I swear the air has such skillful teeth some nights.

But on this dear shore, lapping rime and grace,
There's security tonight with inaccuracies
Alone, that old business of nothing but
Calm ahead, impatience with another
As a voice flies into me,
Telling us, go soon.

On Going Down Again

Rejoice and beware in the same breath,
But don't hold it too long.
                                        Looking both ways
First, you take me by the ears like a small boy
Being led to Beethoven. I applaud
All the ways we were counted lucky,
Being in the thick of it, in the throes
Of old cold habits. A piece of you
Tells your heart this is the absolute
Last time you set down, invariably lost
To the rise of a ten-hour night
Above the North Atlantic. Hold the sweetness.
Hold your tongue. Over water all evening,
I have come to love the laws of fire.

On Being Out Here

Waiting out here for the rain alone
you don't like being shined on
in back of a five-seat taxi sitting
on the rim of East Jesus, Asia.
You resist counting on the moon
to be slung low, inevitably a tender buttock,
and decide instead on talking down
all the stars you conceive tonight,
as if an ethic. You say: Driver,
take the shortest way to Recluse Bay,
a black gin, and the inexpressible.
It's the very question of shade and water
that results in seizure, a blindness
that leaves you sprawled among glitterings
of yourself in transit. Down Ice House Road,
it's possible all the soft, dark matters
you keep warm, and accumulating, and blooming,
will become you, become this heart
made to order, to melt, compete, race, endure.
Yes, no, or maybe so? All distraction
out here, no directions. So you deepen
the gaze infinitely, eyeball a tiny stillness.
In the Territories some Tuesday,
you will tell yourself more than you ever know—
being completely honest, urgently wrong.

Hong Kong

On Being Out There

Each time you vanish a little more,
lasting as if a lengthening shadow of rain.

Figuring out the fastest way back,
your face turns old as dance itself.
The larger mistake, still too small
to serve as a conditioning event,
trades in the balmy dream of being out there,
forever, at times. You are always welcome
elsewhere, except when singing
counts. You become the habit, come alive
to willful flourishing. Yet mind you,
nothing is as venerable as it could have been.
This evening, strung out with impatience,
ends with foreign laughter, flagging
at the foot of Geary Street, another sunrise.
During this fleeting condition of light,
the game deepens. My outsides ache. The heart's
all decision and digestion. Either burn on
or turn down. I'm just six hours back
and already plush in the arms of Turk Murphy's
Bayside jazz, arguing the lovely omissions
with which I construct my latest dossier.

Don't start anything until I return,
I said, impaired by criteria
of the other world, here alone,
immaculate in disappearance.

San Francisco

For Drunks, in the Nighttime

"That's OK, buddy, You can smoke if you want. I just put up the sign for drunks in the nighttime."
—Minneapolis cab driver

to lost friends
on a blue burn

Sometimes you just go dead in your pants,
Some grand accommodation
Pulled full measure. Sometimes the blood

Goes to stew in midnight's double-boiler,
Some fine seasoning
Toward seizure. Now it's become a thing:

You stranded beyond Third Avenue,
No belly for success;
You slipping from puddle to odd puddle

Of light far up the snaggletoothed street,
Irredeemably wrong,
Gone the lost way of clever patois.

Gallant talk trickles down your shirt,
Your insufferable love
For inquest and truth boils to a leer.

So what about those incursions of mind-loss
Through fields of therefore;
Such cautious inaccuracies; your magic slate?

Sometimes you come alive, newly armed
With a tolerable alibi
For having slept all day on your tie,

Having had your fill of chin music,
One more layer of skin
Peeled off a badly distended lower lip.

Your dancing moons and racing clouds
All throw shadow
As bargain relief to high wind. What's now?

Another game's afoot: you slipping nets
Of well-wishes: you
Walking on sticks, building with rage,

So artfully incomprehensible, absorbed,
So risen like the smoke
Of body heat. Take a month's night rain,

Your eyes wet and difficult, a song
For the world foreknown.
Case-hardened, first time before the last.

You begin obscurity again, in a kiss
Concerning incidentals,
In the coming hours, blue burning blue.

Haunts

Blood sausage hung in Sunday's easy market,
A skin of dust on everything. . . . A few clouds
Of ancient believings
Cruise here like flatirons, while others separate,
Infiltrate like mother's milk . . . one cloud,
An elaborate stain, if you will,
Gains confidence, and some infant's life story
Is told again, its adventures
Distilled like rain about to fall.
In the first steam of day, noontime swelter,
Nothing but predicaments of nickle-dime sex
As the world again unbuttons itself
To age spots, skin folds, stretch marks
Of life quickly aged as if in a barrel
Of prime oak, flame-cured on the levee.
It's down this way the weather conspires
To make a lie of all we know:
Your hair tied in a neat chignon:
Me, talking shipwrecks; you, making
the familiar gesture that is prelude to speech,
Exhaling smoke that drifts, unravels
As discourse, several gauges thicker
Than a good cleaver. Honey,
I'd kiss you flat-out if not hard enough
In this mean, muddy season
Of mutual escape. I'd dedicate this day
To "Jazz for Girls Only," as the sign says,
If that would help set us right or remove
The dead weight of nightlife before lunch.
Crossed with rain, river art sells
Like hot fudge, like us—making scenes,
Pretending destination, forever an arm's length
Of blue apart. There is an afternoon patio
Lush with shadow and form we soon leave
As sauces bubble, bisques thicken,

And a tamper-resistant promise
Is kept. However indistinct, or fixed in place,
Perhaps knotted end-to-end, we are first
The absence of shade, our lone relief.
No one can leave without the river knowing.
No one misses runaway clouds,
Gathering as relics, proof of unprecedented dreams

New Orleans

The Body and Its Borders

All that sweet pushing and the brain gone cold
To another faceless frontier crossing,
Another passing freighter
On whose constant intercessions
We rely for help.

Ours is a bad bit of timing: so caution
If we stray to a softer part of the universe,
Where the lyric tongue outruns feeling.

Never were we so beside the point
Or beyond recovery from the bong
Of a bedspring. Never so
Completely ornamental. Evidently the soul,
Properly sized and occupied,
Still submits to the staggering costs
Of a sunset . . . a serious wink.

I want to slide out from underneath it all
Before you feel something slip,
Some helpless remembering
Of harbor, church, palace, crib.

Ah, roll, abide, penetrate, loiter.
There's always more time to gaze
Into the wreck of the last clear autumn
Of your life become a kind of heaven,

Or into the clutch that far-off one I loved
With the big blind bones,
A stink of fear still stalking my skin. . . .

So it is now that our daring nothings
Keep us knee-deep in tulips,
Keep us whacking against the elements

Keep us in want of being in touch
With tremblings and glories of an older sort.

Four Themes on a Variation

Love

While nothing satisfies, not morning's
Bleary mirror or the slick embrace at hand,
Consider our mutual jewel an untouching, a pouring
Into sweet emptied arms called worth and habit.
Hey, you there, change of mind, eh?
So, it is these comic-book poses that promise
Softer years, quite bearable as amnesia or sex.

Sex

Tough talkers, their brain-pans fried black
From a constant heat, turn out swell
On the boulevard strolling in evening wear.
Appearances being unavoidable
As the urge to keep tuned, even stars
Seems to itch for more, for a squeeze
Of all our drizzling nothings, save time.

Time

Leaning out from this wayside planet,
You witness another life blown like glass
Without pattern or fatuous secret,
Yet a limited edition of uncertain radius.
Presume then to be home, a part dismantled
By continuity; some guiding light
Phasing on and off like an unoriginal religion.

Religion

Get far up and hard in the hole
Between dead-of-winter skies and beyond
Limits of ourselves documented by precinct,
Greeted cordially by scandal. Too soon
Allegiance becomes resistance and otherwise;
Meanwhile, after a holy pinch in the ass
You are often saved and, perhaps, in love.

Double-Dare Dreams at the Hotel Amsterdam

Niet storen

A few old bloods puddle perfectly
On this stumbling block of a night table,
Connecting to faint, ancient frequencies
That bubble up through this blue hour
And later appear as tattoos I can't explain.

* * *

There's evening again, tumbling out of its sleeve,
A wet edge, a sweat, an underseas poetry telling me
I did not end in heated argument at the alehouse;
I did not sing a history of the skin-trade;
I did gesture wildly with my father's mahlstick;
I did not submit to any sacral hush;
I did not share the last of my jugged hare;
I did not make night repairs at your polder;
I did not find faith at the Sherry Bodaga;
I did not see anything out of time's order;
I did not buy the hard sell of God, either.

So how long did I listen to de Witte's painted lady
Play mournfully on the clavecin?
And to where did the two of us finally repair?

* * *

In mufti, I keep gathering a need for evidence
Of the deepening twilight, that borderless territory
Of shadows unresolved along the breakwater,
Where it appears that art becomes random
And life requires ransom. . . . Likewise,
I begin to believe in sequences: a clutch
Of yellow songs about a forgettable science
In an age we might possibly survive.

* * *

Dream of children crying their way out of summer.
Dream of them recklessly eyeballing
A night lost to its own sudden history.
How the semi-articulated light in autumn
Bathes, forms, probes in sharp relief
The minimum-wage face. They know,
Too, the sound of bolting and double-bolting
The unfound door of night. Dream the children
Now laughing at the ways of Heaven cast down
On the moon-frozen road to Utrecht,
In a time growing colder and shorter.
Dream the Bourgeois Anonymous
Floating candlelike in the foul canal,
The water still black with ducks,
The ducks awaiting crumbs from children.
Both ducks and children the short stories
Of flesh. Both children and ducks
Wonder why it has been winter for ever
So long and never exactly Christmas.

* * *

Ahead, this endless duplication of interiors
And plump figures disappearing through gabled doors,
Behind drapes, down corridors,
Into the angular depths of mirror
Facing mirror, into my hypnotic shimmer,
All in distemper, a candidate for rupture.

Behind me, skin and wine, more composure
Under that bare stone moon. So a jenever
For luck, so a bloody spit for the sewer.
Nearsighted, I call it prayer and pour
Another treatment, another long hour
Marking time in the name of the Old Sailor.

* * *

In a twinkling,
This night draws water,
Then sinks
As if a ship erased from registry.
I wake, vanishing
Among donnage,
When a great cleverness sets in.
So I go low
And show how the dead
In bed are blessed
By following seas.

I can't protect my dying
In Amsterdam.
I can't shield the lie
I tell from a true,
Certain memory or me:
Up since dawn
One fashionable night
Soon going down
In desparate wetness
Near the Spui,
Heart come apart
A dirty last time
From sleep, from water's
Nudge. So then
The bottle gets flung,
The switch thrown,
The clock stopped,
The letting-go gone,
All those facts against me.

I concentrate
To blankness. Hover among women
And other shadings; taste

Reality's lipstick;
Kiss hello
Another dream without end.

Crossings: November 21-22

for Dana Gioia

Chicago—Paris, the business again,
and again all the high-order reasoning
of night flight takes hold as we shed coat,
trade smiles, stow gear, ease down, shake hands,
latch table, stretch out, rub feet, buckle up,
talk small, pop mint, press light, and bless self
while instructed in the rites of safety,
and all cabins cross-checked, prepared for departure,
and all of us brought to a full, upright
and locked position as we rumble down
the runway lifting off into roseate twilight
and jet stream, hung out, exhausted, gone. And soon,
we become part of the going rate—climbing
yet fixed, floating too predictably.
Thus, we assume elevation's space and, sooner,
bumps from things in the night. And soon enough,
all the rich meats of Air France run bloody
and cool, duck bonne femme muddled
in peppercorn sauce, spoils of Madagascar,
another freshly boned truth to feed upon.
So we're up and outrunning vibration,
banking through a touch of turbulence,
head winds seemingly deep and fluent as tides.
So we too become matters for complex negotiation,
due diligence, higher net worth.
As we smooth to new cruising altitude,
I level off with an Armagnac and faint smile
from the long-legged woman across the aisle,
maybe headed the way of strangers and dangers,
an idea left unbuttoned as imagination.
Just now she leans over to whisper:
"When leaving the country these days, don't
forget to put a stop-loss on your portfolio. . . ."

It occurs to me at 40,000 feet we count
too much upon implausible returns. With any luck
unwinding empty in a suit, it's conceivable
I've had enough of the plentiful stuff
of which schemes are made—capital ventured,
offers tendered. Tonight, queuing up
alongside stars, I rifle my briefcase
for other game, for poems, and in the black
of this blue interception find you and yours,
blessings and lessons for flying cloud legends,
somehow collecting time while spending it.
This is straight time I'm doing, doing
a subtitled movie before lights out.
And the 747 surges, hums itself into a lullaby
for those hundreds now sleeping, slack-jawed,
blankets tucked, spittle on chins,
twitching from an occasional love instinct,
a few hands slaving under covers,
all through this soft doze in the muff of space.
Out of porthole, patroling the night watch
for death winds or a perfect prayer,
I write, "Love demands the slipstream night,
the flight in which you ride it, and it
rides you, until what happens, happens,"
into another notebook from another ocean crossing.

So I'm mid-Atlantic and forty years into a life
official as a passport, equally unquestioned;
me, gaining critical mass and balance,
if only in the spirit of a midcourse correction.
Nearing dateline, darkness soon to be day,
I remember John Kennedy shot dead
decades ago tomorrow or tonight, whichever;
Kennedy eternally dying on film,
America exploded in black and white,

America crying to "God Bless America,"
collapsing into myth, proposition, dilemma,
a distant bygone, as if spilled milk.
I'm still glazed, utterly. Memories await
exquisite remaking as institutional history. Ha,
big money still costs way too much. Ha,
we still believe the world so rich
one ought to cheat more than a bit. So go
such dim arguments of generations
set loose and lost upon each other. I think,
keep the dark shining and those sermonettes
irrelevant. Too many of us are still missing
in action, unable to finance a memorable warmth.
Inklings of a bad moon rising whenever
I'm part of the sky. Grindings of expectation
whenever I'm sitting pretty. How I marvel
at last at the unravelings I count
as liabilities of your average hopefulness.
So many slogans of revolution, half-turned loves
returned to me tonight, like projections,
still reminding of what to believe in in America:
our jazz, our wildness, all our unresolved
lumps still bubbling up through melting pots. . . .

Ah, foraging on the run, on the circuit,
in the necessitarian thick of cost
containment, competitive advantage, 3-D
spread sheets, and tiered-contribution analysis.
At times afraid of flying this high, this fast,
this hard, I reflect on deals struck
and done and see only myself staring out
the black oval, blinking back
at new-found stars, counting my ways
a part of such inconclusive, ongoing
presentlessness, immeasurably alone

with my own retellings, private traces,
elations, hesitations, realignments, and more.
How I love this window-shopping for soul,
for each piece of heaven's fancy,
for some better way to muscle history,
for taking possession of my own remains
and knowing what to make of them. I shift
positions and guess there's sloppy weather
ahead, as the plane twists beyond midnight,
inveigling, intransitive, intractable.
In no time we'll dip toward a distinct line
of dove-gray sky, horizon cut
into darker flannel, the clearing edge
of earth unending. In this dead stretch,
I greet myself halfway across the sky,
whether an initiative or erasure.
It might help to understand my reluctance
to be earthed or sucked forth by speed
that punctures every safe reserve of this
blinking-blanking world I've secured
as if a loan. Just take me away, nose up,
lavishly thankful for all I see that goes
blessedly unsaid. I know events
necessarily outrace strategies; assets
perform accordingly, as if miracles.
Rubbing hands in anticipation of who-knows-what,
some life of spill and hurry, I harbor
no hard feelings for the rimes of our times:
grim and trim; persuasion as evasion; fake songs
and wrong mistakes. Do we require rescue
or refuge, moment or episode, from a republic
of pleasure, some Switzerland of interpretation?
I have learned from a distance even fog
holds a cutting edge; that a mask can be worn
on the groin, how weather is nearly essential.

Someone coughs. It's Friday night
over Halifax and quite early tomorrow
down in the skinhead dawn of downtown Belfast.

Someone still thinks it's an age when loneliness
figures to be as repetitive as it is
decorative, when market forces are still
as purely coincidental as freedom's twitch.
I prefer all of this peculiar space
and its incurable view. Such is order
and strangeness. Such will be continuation.
I ride the good ride Air France provides,
coming alive to descent, discontinuing monologue
with the bulkhead, surrendering earphones,
unused. I'm cheerful this hazy morning aloft,
bearing down upon Europe; for now, seamless
in either skin or sky. There's Paris
in autumn morning haze, iced by rain
before first welcome. Sunrise blocked,
but nonetheless a light source dispassionate
as we swing into final approach
to the desires of Paris just waking
when it is almost winter and before-hours.
I think there's enough time left to avoid
repentence, to sell originality as insurance,
to establish interests in the name of fiasco,
to pain and wretch among our borrowings.
By noon I'll be in conference on Rue St. Honore;
by eight, asleep over dinner at Guy Savoy.
This is as stunning as the future becomes.

SIXTH

Walking the Blind Dog

1 *Dark & Co.*

However you need it to be, it's different
Behind the fine edge of our leanings,
Wind-aided, and us reeling halfway home.
Compare and beware,
                    your agenda and mine,
Each laid before us like barrier reef:
One given to night's clarifications;
Another worried the dark might collapse
With its full weight.
                    Obediently wandering
On short leash, we can stagger elsewhere
If you wish, through sentimental empty spaces,
Through an old chilled ooze in the skull,
Full of our others,
                    yet suctioned apart.
Be patient and be quick. And move unannounced,
Whether by appetite or infection. See here,
More will be known between and about us,
Making the rounds.
                    You halt first and resume,
Until we sweep in like infantry, reclaiming
All the pleasures we cannot help being,
All the ways we cover such wild distances.
Ah, my ripe friend,
                    we turn cold, fugitive
Again, spirited prowlers of the here and now,
Edging out toward that slick black absence
Of everything evening is willing to concede.

2 *Hair of the Dog*

I love these double puzzlements,
The guessing and whispering,
Whenever a huge night takes to the run.

I love being so completely disposed
To salvage. And I love such release,
Coasting at odds, whether to fetch or sic,

Only to see now how we come by those stars
You ignore, moving face down, gone
To the wake of the moon's last hangover.

Remember, inside, we might be Friday again,
Closer to new clearance, nearer the end,
The whole genius of chase torn by your will.

Long afterward, plain drunk, some buried eye
Lurks indistinct and wide as winter.
Afterthought? No. Just a prayer for snow.

3 *Switchback Tales*

Here's to having more mud flung in sorry eyes,
More forced marches, two-steps, shuffles,
Practice waltzes. Here's to being dead sure
Your path remains elegant
In zigzag walks down in Lime Walk
Or some tumble-off to the Middle Region.
It's often a trail sorted out by scents,
But with no clue as how to return
To where a lasting stare reveals safe-home.
Make no mistake: In passing out
Into pitchfork rain, giving interval,
You strain at air between us,
Elevations beyond us. Switchback then
And linger, discover the going rate,
Some eventual music, as you fade empty
Of sight, but always overtake the far shade.

4 *Retrievals*

Deny us if you can. Debate logistics
And dislocation, harrowing runs and maneuvers
In a hollow. No matter. It's more grime
For the fairway, between ditches, slowing fast
From portico to exit, through pond
To exquisite fogbank and farther,
Ever in tow, still foraging for accident
Or resolution. Your leash goes slack
And evening turns cowardly
In the face of another lake's pure
Imagination. Time for the unacceptable
Again, taking on acres of indecision,
Straying across fields just now far short
Of old stone places. Pity
These travels of a one-trick dog,
No longer a necessity. Pity the unguided
Missile wary of its own impulse.

5 *Ear as Eye*

Hear the possibilities of a countervailing wind.
Listen to the way it looks to me now and then.

Twist, and again spin. Let up until you're better
Acquainted with night and its second thoughts.

Absently, with fixed grin and cocked leg,
You choose brambles over pavement, prefer

Escape to rescue. Whoever proves kind and legal
Can blame both the seductions and warrants

Of midnight. Stay on guard. The compulsory stunts
Aren't right. So the ear must become the eye.

Here, below October, when early breeze displays
Its skills as a privilege, we run to catch

Our death in choices, as ever. Come now,
But ready for traps. Let's inherit what's hungry!

6 *Free-Form in the Bottom Land*

How strange to dearly stride out
Into things, out of control,
Stumble against weather
And your failed instincts.
                                        Like a flashlight,
The institutional memory
Clicks on and off.
Who leads who?
Whose right in the way?
                                        Like suture
Dissolving, we hang on
Before stretching
Beyond reach, without much damage,
Game for an eternity of rude astonishments.

7 *Night Moves*

What we need now is a recognition that we are not
Anywhere yet. Drag and step, step and drag
That uncertain leg.
                                        Still, night moves and beckons
What it chooses. We return to whatever fits
Our territorial splits as you take
To the northern-most borders of our murmuring,
A coolness from words. There's always giggling
At the heart of argument, in opposition
To even a honeyed taste of summer's demise.
What's your side of any story?
                                        Out for only air,
Say, we feel our way among luxuries of pebble,
Gathering leaves, this late collection of lawns.
That was it: Us and inevitable traces
Of track before us, holding on against passage
And decay, then the unlistening, comic poses
By a laurel bush, local signs and louder gulls,
All in jerkwater dance.
                                        In these slim proceedings,
All the light that ever need be shines
On our singularity, under the influence
Of a farewell sky and its whims
Until we tremble again . . . stand blessed again.
Once more we concentrate a search, make haste
Toward lappings of rime and place, uninterrupted,
But crying out loud, on the Flats. So do
What you are told and I'll confirm the same,
However long morning after yesterday's remembering.

8 *Saturday Night and Sunday Morning*

Let us now proclaim the mysteries of our faith,
Resurrections of the would-be dead,
Those wandering few, drifters out of time,
Rendered true: moon-stars so far
From you, but clear, and night-tangled
Like a mane, tossed to shining tides
In an unmeasured field, in wider orbit.
Here we are breathing deeply together
For good, for laughs, no looking back
On the cold wastes we entertain endlessly.

Forgive us our haunts. Forgive us our trespasses.

9 *This Far This Night*

Hurtle on, down and back, storms on the line.

And then, to what end? If whiskey-brown eyes
That surround us, mean to immerse us,
Then we perform as two movements: shifting moods
Of night's next day, irregular launchings
And demarcations. It all gets louder,
This ferment in the lungs, the belly, the brain.
Give me a vector. You're coming home,
Pardoned, alive to one well-preserved bark,
Howling to film reel of what's left of us,
Plunging out toward insinuations
Of shoal, washed up to shallows we call,
Basically, the hell of it. . . .

Until rope runs out
Until walking begins night again

Poetry from Illinois

History Is Your Own Heartbeat
Michael S. Harper (1971)

The Foreclosure
Richard Emil Braun (1972)

The Scrawny Sonnets and Other Narratives
Robert Bagg (1973)

The Creation Frame
Phyllis Thompson (1973)

To All Appearances: Poems New and Selected
Josephine Miles (1974)

The Black Hawk Songs
Michael Borich (1975)

Nightmare Begins Responsibility
Michael S. Harper (1975)

The Wichita Poems
Michael Van Walleghen (1975)

Images of Kin: New and Selected Poems
Michael S. Harper (1977)

Poems of the Two Worlds
Frederick Morgan (1977)

Cumberland Station
Dave Smith (1977)

Tracking
Virginia R. Terris (1977)

Riversongs
Michael Anania (1978)

On Earth as It Is
Dan Masterson (1978)

Coming to Terms
Josephine Miles (1979)

Death Mother and Other Poems
Frederick Morgan (1979)

Goshawk, Antelope
Dave Smith (1979)

Local Men
James Whitehead (1979)

Searching the Drowned Man
Sydney Lea (1980)

With Akhmatova at the Black Gates
Stephen Berg (1981)

Dream Flights
Dave Smith (1981)

More Trouble with the Obvious
Michael Van Walleghen (1981)

The American Book of the Dead
Jim Barnes (1982)

The Floating Candles
Sydney Lea (1982)

Northbook
Frederick Morgan (1982)

Collected Poems, 1930-83
Josephine Miles (1983)

The River Painter
Emily Grosholz (1984)

Healing Song for the Inner Ear
Michael S. Harper (1984)

The Passion of the
Right-Angled Man
T. R. Hummer (1984)

Dear John, Dear Coltrane
Michael S. Harper (1985)

Poems from the Sangamon
John Knoepfle (1985)

Eroding Witness
Nathaniel Mackey (1985)
National Poetry Series

In It
Stephen Berg (1986)

Palladium
Alice Fulton (1986)
National Poetry Series

The Ghosts of Who We Were
Phyllis Thompson (1986)

Moon in a Mason Jar
Robert Wrigley (1986)

Lower-Class Heresy
T. R. Hummer (1987)

Poems: New and Selected
Frederick Morgan (1987)

Cities in Motion
Sylvia Moss (1987)
National Poetry Series

Furnace Harbor: A Rhapsody
of the North Country
Philip D. Church (1988)

The Hand of God and
a Few Bright Flowers
William Olsen (1988)
National Poetry Series

Bad Girl, with Hawk
Nance Van Winckel (1988)

Blue Tango
Michael Van Walleghen (1989)

The Great Bird of Love
Paul Zimmer (1989)
National Poetry Series

Eden
Dennis Schmitz (1989)

Waiting for Poppa at the Smithtown Diner
Peter Serchuk (1990)

Great Blue
Brendan Galvin (1990)

Stubborn
Roland Flint (1990)
National Poetry Series

What My Father Believed
Robert Wrigley (1991)

Something Grazes Our Hair
S. J. Marks (1991)

The Surface
Laura Mullen (1991)
National Poetry Series

Walking the Blind Dog
G. E. Murray (1992)